My Bum's on THE RUN!

Dawn McMillan

Illustrated by Ross Kinnaird

SCHOLASTIC

Today is **race** day!
I'm here at the start.

I **SO** want to win –
I have hope in my heart.

I'm ready. . .

I'm steady. . .

And off I go!

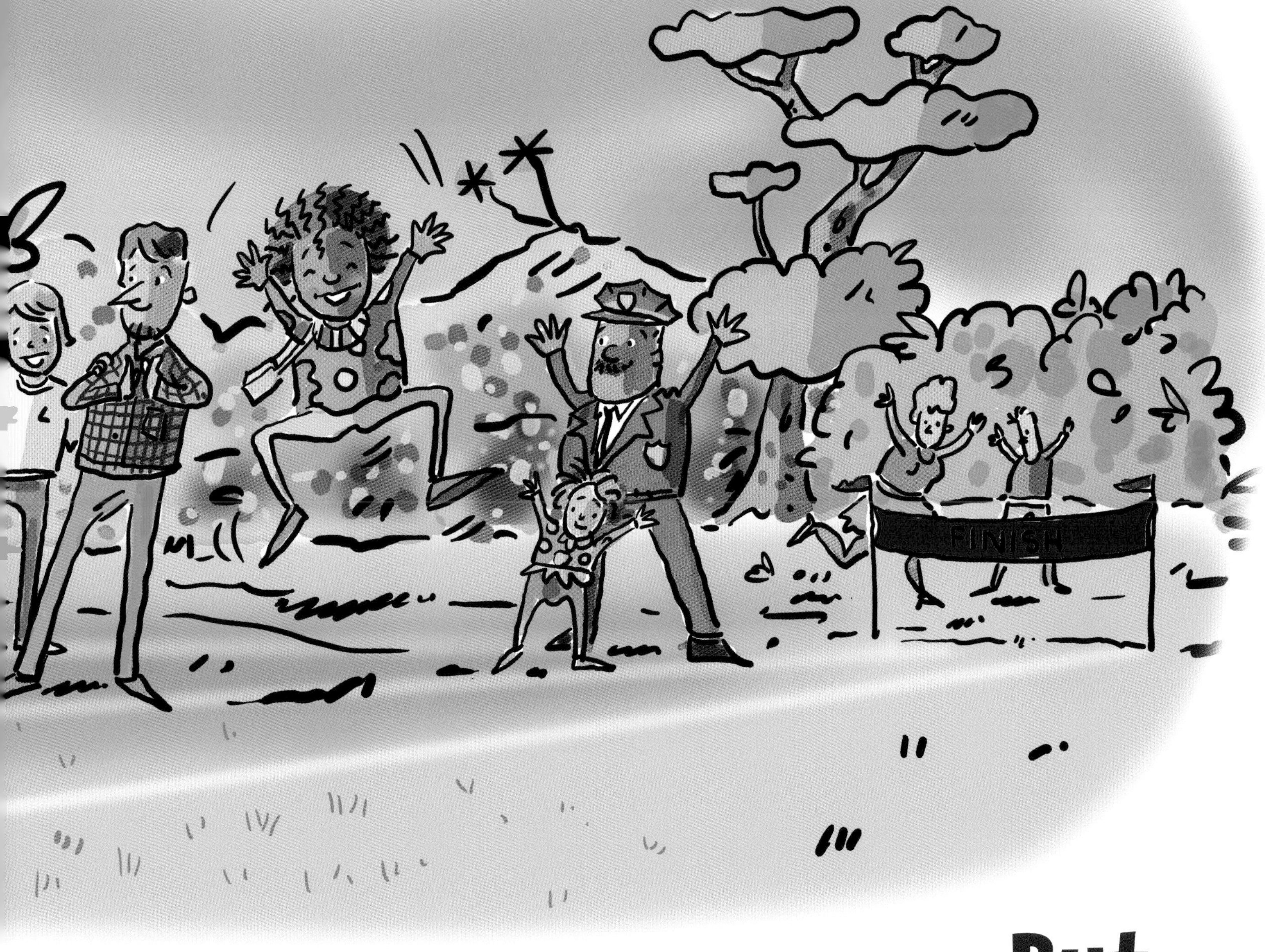

But . . .

. . . I'm coming last because
my bum is so s-l-o-w.

My legs are long.
My knees are **strong**.
But my bum needs something
to move it along.

Like ...

...A **BIG** engine that makes a jet

ROAR.

Or a high-flying kite to make my bum *soar*.

Balloons perhaps,
tied all about.

They will propel me
when the air **rushes** out.

Or a rocket bum **BLAST** – I wouldn't come last!

And if I was followed by *bees* my bum would run **FAST!**

My cousin is Tom,
he has race **trouble** too.
"Cousin," I say,

"I know what to do."

I know that squats
are good for our bots.

And kicks

here and **there**,

with one leg in the air.

Yes, steps **up** and steps **down** –
1, 2, and 3, 4.

A **lunge** and a **plunge** . . .
and then we do it some more.

There's the odd little slip up
that sounds like a **hiccup**.
But what's that we hear?
Is it a **cheer**?

There's whooping and hollering.
Seems we have a following.

WHAT A HULLABALOO.

They're having fun too!

So now Tom and I, we go running for **fun**.
Down the footpath, along past the trees
I'm out in front, moving with ease.
(With my new **secret** weapon –

cabbage and peas!)

And I know . . .

My bum could run **FAST**
in all sorts of races
all over the world,
in wonderful places.

Like . . .

Through city streets and on riverbanks too.

Along the tall cliffs with the best view.

A **mud** run perhaps,
a race in the **rain**.

Around the lake shore, and back again.

A race in the desert?
Now that would be **fun**.
With a **strong** bum that could be done.

In **COLD** places to go
    I could race in the *snow*.

I could race high, right up to the sky.

To race by the sea would really suit me.

Yes . . . I'd like to be famous.

A world **racing** star!

But my bum isn't keen to travel too far.

So . . .

Tom and I enter a cross country race.

Over **hills** and through **streams**,

near our home place.

And I'm over the gate! But Tom's running late!
Along a farm track! I'm too near the back!

I need more **grunt** to get to the front.

The line's up ahead! My bum is **RED!**

My muscles are *pumping!* My bum is *jumping!*

A dash for the line. My bum's feeling **fine**.

And . . .

... yes!

My bum can run! My bum has WON!

Well, not quite so I hear...

Guess who has won by the *tip* of his **ear**?

About the author

Hi, I'm Dawn McMillan. I'm from Waiomu, a small coastal village on the western side of the Coromandel Peninsula in New Zealand. I live with my husband Derek and our cat, Lola. I write some sensible stories and lots of silly stories! I love creating quirky characters and hope you enjoy reading about them.

About the illustrator

Hi. I'm Ross. I love to draw. When I'm not drawing, or being cross with my computer, I love most things involving the sea and nature. I also work from a little studio in my garden surrounded by birds and trees. I live in Auckland, New Zealand. I hope you like reading this book as much as I enjoyed illustrating it.

Published in the UK by Scholastic, 2023
1 London Bridge, London, SE1 9BG
Scholastic Ireland, 89E Lagan Road, Dublin Industrial Estate, Glasnevin, Dublin, D11 HP5F

SCHOLASTIC and associated logos are trademarks and/or registered trademarks of Scholastic Inc.

First published in New Zealand by Oratia Media, 2023

Text © Dawn McMillan, 2023
Illustrations © Ross Kinnaird, 2023

The right of Dawn McMillan and Ross Kinnaird to be identified
as the author and illustrator of this work has been asserted by them under the Copyright, Designs and Patents Act 1988.

ISBN 978 0702 32273 0

A CIP catalogue record for this book is available from the British Library.

Printed in Italy
Paper made from wood grown in sustainable forests and other controlled sources.

1 3 5 7 9 10 8 6 4 2

This is a work of fiction. Names, characters, places, incidents and dialogues are products of the author's imagination or are used fictitiously. Any resemblance to actual people, living or dead, events or locales is entirely coincidental.

www.scholastic.co.uk